Each Step I Take

Lila Dooley

Each Step I Take, Published June, 2016

Cover Design: Howard Johnson

Interior Design & Layout: Howard Johnson, Howard Communigrafix, Inc.

Editorial & Proofreading: Lisa Akoury-Ross, Marie Dooley

Photo Credits: iStock by Getty Images: Young Woman in White Dress, #28339498, © Maria Dubova

 **SDP Publishing**

Published by SDP Publishing, an imprint of SDP Publishing Solutions, LLC.

SDP Publishing
Permissions Department
PO Box 26, East Bridgewater, MA 02333
or email your request to info@SDPPublishing.com.

ISBN-13 (print): 978-0-9972853-5-2

Library of Congress Control Number: 2016943628

Copyright © 2016, Lila Dooley

Printed in the United States of America

Dedicated to all kids
who have been bullied
or feel the way I did.

Contents

PART 1
DARKNESS

PART 2
LIGHT

PART 1

DARKNESS

Darkness

Darkness is the bad path
Yet so many follow
Once you go in there
There's no coming out
The darkness eats away at you
Until you're nothing
There's always that choice
Good or bad
I made the wrong one

Popular

Popular is the thing that separates kids

The popular are the most important

Then it's the sub-popular who try to be popular

After that are miners who aren't important

Then there are the weird kids who are used to make
the popular feel good about themselves

That is where I am

Talking

Talking is something that doesn't really matter

It's not like people are going to remember

So I found that not talking is easy

No one will remember that conversation

It's not like that conversation will change something

Sleep

When I sleep I cry
When I think of tomorrow I cry
When I sleep I have a nightmare
But realize its reality
I wake up and cry

Shadows

Shadows are swallowing me up
They are making me go into that corner
People laugh
People laugh at me
Shadows swallow me up more
I was never me
I was the person they made me
Shadows swallow me up more
I was never invited
I feel like death

One Year Ago

One year ago
My life was hell
People built me up to break me down
I felt like a new kid
One year ago
No one noticed
The pain they brought me
Not only to me but others
To my friends
To my family
I will never forgive them for the pain
The suffering
The tears

I Can Never

I can never be important
I can be pushed aside
I can never be
Just me

Listen

Listen to my voice
I am standing right here
I can't keep yelling
Or all it would be is a whimper
Please hear my voice I am calling
Help me
Please

Labeled

Why do people label?
They labeled me as the weird kid
I had no say
Why cause misery?
Why cause hate and depression?
They could have saved me from those feelings
But where's the fun in that?
For years I lived with it
I felt like I was living a life not worth fighting for
They made me the person in the corner, a shadow
They saw my flaws not me
They don't know the tears I have shed because of them
When seeing someone, know the damage of labels

Bravery

They tell me to be brave

I can't

If I can barely cry 'cause I ran out of tears

So how can I be brave?

If I can't cry away the pain

If I can't even talk with my head up

I Wish

I wish to take away pain
The pain that my family endured
The tears we have shed are endless
The smiles are few
I remember my mom's face
Every time I bared bad news
If only
I could do something right

Frozen

Looking around at the frozen wasteland
The one that connects the land and sea
I see this from my window
The one that overlooks everything
Where the ice dances around on the surface
I was standing frozen in fear
Of what's to come

You Think

You think I'm happy
but i'm not

You think I'm weak
That is true

You think I'm invisible
That's right

You think I'm stupid
I can't argue

You think I don't hear you
I do

You think I don't notice
But I can

You think I don't cry
I cry every day

You think I don't notice the whispers
I count them

You think I'm nobody
I am

Night

I am night

I am fear

I am the thing that goes away

I am the one in the shadows

I am the one that makes everyone afraid

Just because I live in the shadows doesn't mean

I am not there

I still hear

I still think

I still love

I still run

But you can't run away from your shadow

People

Why do people not notice things?
They take things for granted
They never notice until it's gone

PART 2

LIGHT

Each Step I Take

Each step I take leads a different way

Each step I take is to a different adventure

Each step I take is only going further

Each step I take adds to a mile

Each mile I take

I smile

Snowflake

The little snowflake that was different

The one that falls in a different path

The one that stands out among the others

The one that is different...

But if you stand out that just means you're
beautiful

The little snowflake that brought beauty into...

The snow

But unlike all the others

This snowflake is unique

But unique doesn't always mean odd

Together

Together we shall live

Together we shall cry

Together we shall fall

Together we shall rise

Together we will fly up to the clouds

I Am Not

I am not one to speak in groups

I am not one to make you think a certain way

I am not one to make someone's life a living hell

I am not one to get angry

I am not one to speak true feelings

But...

Who am I?

I am quiet

I am nervous

I am happy

I am one who lives life in the present

I am unbroken

I am unbreakable

I am me

Life

Life can be bad

But that doesn't mean it's always going to be

You have to have bad times

To make the good stand out

Life can't be forever

We are not immortal

But it's not about the

Hours

Minutes

Seconds

It's about how you spend that time

By the dreams you have

By the people you meet

By the lasting relationships with friends and
family...

That makes us immortal through memories

That is just life

No One

No one can be me
They can try but fail
Only I can be the better me
I can't be the better other person
Only that person can be

Perfect

Perfect is a word to describe ordinary
That's the thing about me
I am not perfect
I am not ordinary
I am extraordinary

Who I Was

I was a wreck

I was on the edge of being broken

I was just another person

I was the last one

I was living in fear

I was a shadow of a smiling face

But that was in the past

I am none of those things

This is the present

This is my life

I am not going back into the shadows

I am one that dances in the light

I am one who will help others dance

Dance in the light with me

Why I Write

I write for fun
I write for experience
I write when in pain
I write for my family
I write for my friends
I write to not forget my past
But most of all
I write for the future of my life

Heart

The heart is the center of your body
To survive you need a heart
To love you HAVE to have a heart

Good or Bad

The good people are the ones who can be soft spoken

The ones who sometimes don't say a word...

But you know what they are thinking

You can tell the good and bad apart with no words...

But actions

The bad people are the ones who need attention

Though it's hard to tell

You'll know when you find them

The good ones

When you find them you'll feel happy

They will accept you for personality

Not popularity

They will not care for who you were

But for who you'll become

I found them this year

Broken

I like to think I have not been broken

But I have

I have been broken many times

I have been broken

Broken into little pieces

They can't break me I won't let them without a fight

I will gather up the pieces to make me whole

I am not letting them build me up to be

Brought down

I am not a toy

To make myself whole

To stay

To be unbroken

The Bird that Stayed

For the bird that stayed for the winter

For the pedals that fall to the sea

For the sea that is a deep blue

For the ice that is like a clear diamond

For the bird that stayed

But winter doesn't mean

Gone

With Friends

With friends I found myself
No, they did more
With friends I created myself
They helped me be whole again
Thought I was not able to make friends anymore
They proved me wrong
I made friends and I love them
They make me laugh no matter what mood I am in
I am with people
I thought every person was bad
Though I have met people
good friends
It was only a few
All of them
They were the people ...
Who saved me from my shadow
They are the best friends in my life

Look

Look into the sky with never ending color

Look for the stars that make the sky complete

Look across to the city, which touches the limitless
sky

Look out to the waves that gently touch your feet

Look down to the shells that match the beauty of the
sun

Look over to the endless beach that holds so many
memories

Look to me to help make more memories

Look forward to seeing this again

Love

Love is never ending

Love you do not know until you feel it

Love is earned not bought

Love is not an item but a thought

Love has no bounds

Love can be in many forms

Love is not a lesson it can't be taught

Love you can't find because it will find you

Love is everything you say and do

Love is the thing we search for but don't recognize
when it's right in front of you

Love is the best part of being human

Love is when I am with you

One

One spark can start a fire
One seed can create a forest
One word can change lives
One deed can save a life
One life can change the world

sky

The sky is limitless

The sky has eternal color

The sky is the thing that touches the earth yet can't
be touched

The sky is filled with warmth and light

The sky is endless adventure

The sky is endless opportunity

The sky is heaven

Wind

Wind comes and goes

Wind can stay 'til dawn

Wind you can't see but can feel its presence

Wind you never stop and notice

Wind you only notice when it's gone

Sunset

Yellow for tomorrow

Orange for a friend I haven't met

Red for anger passing

Blue for the people who have gone astray

Purple for the happiness I am going to have

Acknowledgments

Thanks to ...

All of my friends: best friend, Kate; old friends, Audrey, Flanagan & Flaherty Family; and new friends, Anna, Alex, Emma W., Catherine S., Maggie, Rebecca, Kaitlyn, Ellie, Cynthia, Lindsey and Chloe

All NDA staff

My Publisher and friend, Lisa Akoury-Ross at SDP and her talented designer, Howard Johnson

My family: my mom, dad, Ava, Harry, and my dog Mac

I love everyone so much
Keep loving
Keep smiling because
You're unique

About the Author

Lila Dooley is a thirteen-year-old middle school student from South of Boston. She is a happy, fun seventh grade girl who knows what it's like to be picked last, or to not be included. Lila has experienced bullying from her peers, and was excluded from parties and get-togethers. She realized that this exclusion too was a form of bullying.

Lila likes gardening. She plays field hockey, basketball and volleyball. She has Attention Deficit and Hyperactivity Disorder (ADHD), which impacted her feelings. She felt all alone. When asked what she wants to do with her life, she responds, "helping people." Lila is always aware of her surroundings. If anyone is left sitting alone, she is usually the first to reach out and include them.

Lila began writing on her own as a form of self-therapy. Through her poems, she is able to express her thoughts and feelings about being a teenage girl, the importance of true friendships and how to always have hope. Lila writes from her heart, and hopes that her poetry will help those that have experience with feeling left out or being different. She wants readers to know that they are not alone, others have the same feelings, and this too shall pass. Everyone deserves friends who accept them for their personality, not their popularity.

Each Step I Take
Lila Dooley

Publisher: SDP Publishing

Available at all major bookstores.

 SDP Publishing

www.SDPPublishing.com
Contact us at: info@SDPPublishing.com

CPSIA information can be obtained at www.ICGtesting.com
Printed in the USA
BVOW06s0822020916

460964BV00016B/99/P

9 780997 285352